Electing
to Bat

Electing
to Bat

Tales of glory and disaster
from the Palace of Westminster

Edited and compiled by
Harry Greenway MP

Illustrations by
John Ireland

Queen Anne Press

A QUEEN ANNE PRESS BOOK

© Lennard Associates Limited 1996

First published in 1996 by
Queen Anne Press, a division of
Lennard Associates Limited
Mackerye End
Harpenden, Herts AL5 5DR

A catalogue entry is available from the British Library

ISBN 1 85291 577 3

Production Editor: Chris Hawkes
Cover Design/Design Consultant: Design 2 Print
Reproduction: CMYK Graphics/Leaside Graphics
Printed and bound in England
by Butler & Tanner, London and Frome

CONTENTS

FOREWORD BY
THE PRIME MINISTER
THE RT HON JOHN MAJOR MP

To the popular imagination, cricket and Parliament may not appear to have much in common. Cricket after all is a game for the fair-minded sportsman. A spectator sport which can be enjoyed by all those taking part and all those watching. How different Parliament sometimes can seem. The political parties lined up against each other, engaging in a battle which might appear to be based more on cunning and deviousness than on the rules of fair play.

But that of course is just the surface. Underneath the froth, I believe that politics, like cricket, is still pursued by people of honour and integrity. That is why it is no surprise to me to find that so many of my fellow Parliamentarians share my love of the game.

All those contributing to this book – politicians from both sides of the House of Commons and indeed from the House of Lords – have enjoyed taking part in or watching cricket for many years. Perhaps within the pages of this book will be found the answer to one political mystery, namely what happens to our Parliamentarians during the long summer months when Parliament is in recess.

I have been following the game for almost half a century. Along the way I have witnessed some of the greatest cricketers in action. I have been present at some of the greatest moments in cricketing history.

I was lucky enough, for example, to be there when Colin Cowdrey took a catch at second slip to give Freddie Trueman his 300th Test wicket. I saw Graham Gooch's 333 at Lord's. I remember as a boy listening on the radio to the remarkable May/Cowdrey stand at Edgbaston that finally destroyed the invincible myth of Ramadhin and Valentine.

My own cricket career had rather lower points than this. I remember at school, aged ten, being given out LBW for 0 after a perfectly straightforward defensive stroke in which the ball had hit the middle of the bat. I looked at the umpire in dumbfounded dismay and discovered later in physics lessons that he really was as blind as a bat. I also made my highest-ever score of 77 not out playing for Northern Nigeria at Jos in the mid-1960s. Alas, the possible 100 was wiped out by the mail plane arriving a day early and arriving at square leg. 77 not out – plane stopped play – I bet even Bill Frindall cannot find that happening anywhere else. This sort of thing never happened to Peter May!

The beauty of the game of cricket is that, no matter the level at which it is played, it can produce gripping excitement and enjoyment. As you read through the contributions that follow, you can see how every game carries the potential to keep players and spectators reliving incidents and debating decisions hours after the stumps have been drawn and the sun has gone down.

10 Downing Street
London SW1
October 1996

INTRODUCTION:
CRICKET AND PARLIAMENT

Sir Neville Cardus was much stirred by the sight of Harold Macmillan batting for the Lords and Commons XI during his premiership. During his innings his bat split. Naturally, the Prime Minister immediately had a fresh bat brought from the pavillion and the innings continued. Sitting in his club, Cardus regaled me with the story of another Prime Minister whose bat was similarly split whilst batting at Lords: 'He strode towards the pavillion,' said Cardus, 'waving the bat aloft and shouting "Bring me some more bats!".'

The story reminds us that both MPs and Members of the House of Lords have been interested in, and supportive of, the great game of cricket from its earliest days – both as spectators and players. Constituency selection committees like to choose candidates with good all-round abilities, and, in my opinion, skill and achievement at games and sport do no harm to one's chances of being selected to fight a seat. Most notably, former England captain Ted Dexter, who happens to live on the edge of my own constituency, was chosen to fight for the Conservative Party against the former Prime Minister James Callaghan in his Cardiff constituency. This was at least partly due to his outstanding record for his county and his country at cricket.

At the present time, some one hundred and forty MPs and Members of the House of Lords belong to the All Party Parliamentary Cricket Group. The Group meets monthly, when the House is sitting, to dine and to hear a talk from someone great or important from within the game. Discussions on these evenings are of a very high standard indeed and Members are amazingly well informed as well as being great devotees of the game. Mike Atherton's talk on what it takes to be captain of England has been one of the many highlights; we have also heard from other England players both past and present, county captains, the Secretary of the MCC, overseas players and many more.

In the summer of 1995, the Speaker Betty Boothroyd MP, kindly allowed us to entertain the West Indies team in her State Rooms. This gave us the chance to talk to them all – including Brian Lara, the world record holder for the highest innings in both Test and first-class cricket – informally and without pressure. In 1996 the group entertained both the Indian and Pakistan touring teams in the Churchill Room of the House of Commons. All team members came, and although I cannot say I noticed much, if any, dialogue between the two squads, the opportunity was there. For our part, we were able to pursue our Parliamentary duty to the game and to think more deeply about what needs to be done to improve cricketing opportunities (both watching and playing) for people of all ages. After all, visiting touring teams can make valuable suggestions from their own experiences at home and also from what they notice as they travel around this country playing county and Test cricket.

Do the game of cricket and Parliament have anything in common? Does John Major's well-known passion and knowledge of cricket enhance his performance in the bear pit of the House of Commons? Do the Prime Minister's visits to Test matches gain or lose him electoral support? Some might say that he ought not to have time for this if he is doing his job properly, whilst others will say that his identification with what is a passionate interest of so many others brings him both personal warmth and political support. It is hard to answer such questions, but I am certain that facing up to fast and frightening bowling, fielding close to the wicket or learning how to attack a stubborn or a fluent batsman can only help the Parliamentarian to face those inevitable 'bumpers' and 'shooters' from opponents

'Preparing the Ground'

in the House, not to mention the 'skyers', 'mishits', 'edges', 'smart drives', 'hasty singles' and 'overthrows', with which any Parliamentarian might have to cope. Courage is needed; long- and short-term strategies; confidence and the ability to hang in there when the going is rough. All play their part in both games and a ruling, whether it is from the Speaker or the match umpire, is the final word.

So, would Len Hutton, Don Bradman, Denis Compton, Brian Lara or Mike Atherton have made great Parliamentarians rising to the rank of Cabinet Minister or even Prime Minister? If they are interested, there is still time for Mike Atherton and Brian Lara to show if this can be done, whilst it is unlikely that Denis Compton at eighty, or Sir Donald Bradman at ninety, would still entertain such ambitions. Nonetheless, and speaking as one who has met, talked to and listened to each of these individuals (with the exception of Bradman), I can say that they are, or were, keenly interested in politics; shrewd observers of the game, both in Parliament and outside of it; brilliant PR men; able speakers in public; sharp in wit and wise in the ways and tricks of man. If truly interested, each of them and probably many other cricketers could have had a career in politics and, conversely, many current and former MPs – David Faber, Member for Westbury, for example – could have made a successful life for themselves in cricket as players, administrators, umpires or, most likely of all, as commentators. The marvellous truth is that there much in common between the game of cricket and the Parliamentary game at Westminster.

Harry Greenway MP

'HOW TO WIN VOTES AND INFLUENCE PEOPLE'

I was playing cricket for a team outside my constituency, which had no connection with politics. After scoring a few runs, I was hit in the face by an awkward bouncer and retired, bloody and hurt. I later returned to the crease only to be caught out immediately by the person who had earlier bowled at me. Before I went to the hospital to be stitched up, the culprit admitted that he was one of my constituents.

A few weeks later at a village fete, a lady asked after my health and then admitted that she was the mother of the cricketer. She assured me that, regardless of how he had voted in the past, he and the rest of the family now felt obliged to turn out for me at the next election!

Ian Taylor MBE, MP
Ian Taylor is MP for Esher.

THE FAST BOWLER – A CASE STUDY'
OR 'STUNG INTO INERTIA'

When I was a student at the London School of Economics, the cricket team would finish each season with a tour in Devon. In the year that I was Secretary of the cricket club, I agreed to an additional fixture with one of the Oxford colleges. The game was played at the County Ground at Taunton to coincide with the end of each side's tour.

I soon realised I had made a mistake. Our appearance on the pitch was far from perfect. Putting it bluntly we showed all the wear and tear of a side which had been on tour for over a week. The Oxford college side, on the other hand, was perfectly turned out. Their cricket gear looked as if they had just come from some high-class gents' outfitter. I felt all my natural prejudices against Oxford colleges beginning to assume even greater proportions.

We won the toss and decided to bat. My opening partner was a true son of Sheffield; as such, he also had a view of fast bowlers. Indeed, it was a view which we both shared. Maybe we did not expect the opening bowlers from an Oxford college to have just completed a shift at the local pit. Nevertheless, we did expect fast bowlers to have certain common characteristics. Above all, they should be boorish and aggressive.

Unusually, we made a confident start to our innings. We must have put on about thirty runs when a rare incident took place. I was on strike; the fast bowler was running in to bowl. Halfway through his run up he fell to the ground holding his chest. His team mates rushed to his aid. We had to decide what to do. Should we simply maintain our concentration and acknowledge an inner pleasure in the fact that our opponents had lost their opening bowler; or should we indulge in some social pleasantries and find out what had happened? After a few moments debating we decided to walk across in a steady but concerned manner. We were met by the opposing captain who announced the problem. We had visions of a pulled muscle, a damaged back or any of the injuries which beset fast bowlers, but it was none of these. The captain announced that the fast bowler had been stung on his left breast by a wasp.

Naturally, we were concerned but could not help thinking that in similar circumstances true fast bowlers would have been stung to even greater pace. We could not imagine any of our boyhood heroes being stopped in their tracks as they ran up to bowl for Yorkshire at a packed Bramhall Lane. Our prejudice had been confirmed. Clearly Oxford cricket was soft and southern. It was a good job later in the day that we gave them a sporting declaration so that they had a chance of winning.

Derek Fatchett MP

Derek Fatchett is MP for Leeds Central and was elected in 1983.

'THERE'S A TIME AND A PLACE. . .'

Rather like Sir Francis Drake's alleged game of bowls, my anecdote only coincidentally involves a cricket match. In 1979, a few members of the Conservative Research Department (CRD) team were staying up at Harold Elletson's (now MP for Blackpool North) rather splendid home in North Lancashire. Those playing cricket that Saturday afternoon on the spacious lawn included John Whittingdale (now MP for Colchester South) – he, and Elletson had acted as research assistants and 'runners' during the election campaign; Bruce Anderson (later of *Weekend World* and various national newspapers); Patrick Rock (special adviser to Michael Howard as Home Secretary and before) and myself. During the match I had to take a telephone call from Dermot Gleeson, then acting Director of the Department following Chris Patten's election at Bath (Gleeson went on to a successful business career, principally expanding the family construction company, with a spell in Number 10 before the 1992 election). He told me he had been summoned by Lord Thorneycroft (Conservative Party Chairman), the previous evening, to be told that he (Gleeson) was being replaced by Alan Howarth, then Thorneycroft's personal assistant (later MP for Stratford-upon-Avon and defector to Labour in 1995), and that Howarth was directed to preside over the moving of the quasi-independent CRD from its separate office in Old Queen Street into the Central Office building in Smith Square. This news of the end of an era, in the aftermath of victory, somewhat blighted the cricket and the remainder of the weekend.

David Nicholson MP

David Nicholson is MP for Taunton and was elected in 1987.

'Played and Missed'

'SUMMERTIME BLUES'

When I was an undergraduate at Oxford in the early 1960s, I used to play regular weekend matches for an extremely amateur team known as the Keble Vagabonds.

On one occasion I was playing a local village on a rather cold day and I was bowling in my Oxford boxing Blue sweater. After I had bowled several wides, the elderly umpire took to giving me broad winks as I went back to take up my usual stance bowling left-arm round the wicket. Finally he could contain himself no longer and said in a broad Somerset drawl: 'Surr, when are you going to bowl right-handed?' I realised, then, that he had mistakenly thought I was a cricketing Blue and imagined that I was being kind to the other team in adopting a left-handed delivery!

Sir Nicholas Bonsor, Bt, MP

Sir Nicholas Bonsor was originally elected as MP for Crewe and Nantwich and has been the MP for Upminster since 1983. He has played cricket for Keble Vagabonds and Eton Ramblers.

'A Captain's Innings'

'DIVINE INTERVENTION'

I was playing for my school. The opposing team had a demon bowler who was the terror of the public school circuit. Strong men flinched when taking guard against him. Batting at No.6, I was padded up after our opener had retired hurt from a fearsome bouncer. No.3 was bowled all ends up – more concerned for his physical welfare than the ball. No.4, using his bat to protect his body, was caught at slip.

The sky darkened ominously. A glimmer of hope – could bad light save me? As No.5 walked to the wicket so very slowly, I prayed for rain. Then it came, in torrents... thunder... lightning. Hallelujah! I am saved! Rain stopped play.

That is how I never received a single ball from one who later become a famous Test cricketer – Trevor Bailey.

Sir Anthony Grant MP

Elected MP for Harrow Central in 1964 and for Cambridgeshire South West in 1983, Sir Anthony Grant played cricket for St Paul's School and for the Army whilst serving in the Far East. He was a member of Surrey CCC for many years.

'TALENT SPOTTING'

My grandfather captained Gloucestershire in the 1920s and a history of the club refers to his period in office as the 'years of revival'. It says nothing at all about his cricketing ability as a wicket-keeper/batsman, but does mention that he discovered a 'young man called Hammond'. If he achieved that, then Foster Robinson made a notable contribution to the club and to England – so perhaps modern captains should be subjected to a league table for talent-spotting abilities!

Mark Robinson MP

Mark Robinson is MP for Somerton and Frome, having been elected in 1992. He is a member of the All Parliamentary Cricket Group.

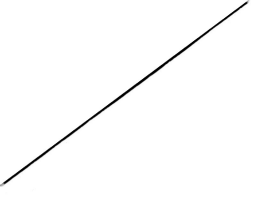

'SECRET WEAPON MISFIRES'

It was not a vintage year for Lords and Commons cricket. The team we marshalled to play against Westminster School was full of foreboding that it would lose. So the captain decided on a secret weapon: he persuaded a former England leg-spin bowler to strengthen the side.

The early opening overs by our rather blunted pace attack caused no problems for the schoolboys. There was no alternative. The first over of leg spin was played respectfully and dutifully back down the pitch. In the second over confidence rose, the ball was pushed firmly for singles. Soon the boys realised they could hit the ball all round the ground for fours. The secret weapon had to be taken off, complaining of a bad shoulder. We lost.

The Rt Hon John Redwood MP

John Redwood is MP for Wokingham and was first elected in 1987. He plays for the Lords and Commons XI.

'The Drinks Interval'

'CORRIDOR OF UNCERTAINTY'

I n the early 1980s I went to the Konrad Adenauer Foundation, Berlin, where the highlight of the visit was a trip to the Berlin Wall. This great monstrosity was covered in graffiti, which, in a curious way, seemed entirely appropriate. One good place to put it! I scanned the various slogans until I found these words written in English: 'Geoff Boycott we love you.'

I recounted this story at Halesowen Cricket Club annual dinner some three weeks later when one wag at the back said: 'Ah, but which side was it written on?'

John M Taylor MP

John Taylor is MP for Solihull and is a member of both the MCC and Warwickshire CCC.

'OVER THE HILL'

At the time at which this took place I was, and still am, President of Adlington Cricket Club who play in the Bolton Association. Playing as professional for Little Hulton, who are also members of the same league, was Mudassar Nazar, the Pakistan Test cricketer, then eighteen years of age.

He had already completed 1,000 runs and taken 100 wickets for the season. When Little Hulton played Adlington he approached me to ask if my club was looking for a professional for next season. 'Yes' I replied. Mudassar said he would like to recommend a colleague of his who played for Pakistan Airways. His colleague was a better all-rounder than he but there was only one snag. He was rather old. When I asked how old he was, he replied: 'Twenty-four.'

Doug Hoyle MP

Doug Hoyle has been MP for Warrington North since 1981. On the cricket field he played for Adlington CC and is now their President. He is a member of Lancashire CCC.

'THE ASHES'

When playing one July at Mottisfont, a small village near Romsey in Hampshire, I arrived a couple of hours before the game to enjoy a picnic with my family. There were thirty or forty people on the square including a vicar. After about twenty minutes the group broke up and most people left the ground. The long-serving groundsman/wicket-keeper made his way off the pitch to open up the pavillion. Having played on the ground for most of the past twenty years I approached him and asked what had been going on.

Dennis replied: 'We got together to remember old Harry. He opened the bowling for us for forty years.' I said that this was a decent thing to do and the groundsman/wicket-keeper agreed. 'We thought it was only right. Mind you, he died in February but he always wanted his ashes spread on the square!'

And indeed, when we went out to play we found the last mortal remains of old Harry spread in grey patches across the square. It was the first game I have ever played in where the spinners did not lick their fingers!

John Denham MP

John Denham is MP for Southampton, Itchen and was elected in 1992. He has played cricket for both Southampton Academicals and the Lords and Commons XI.

'The Demon Bowler'

'How Times Have Changed'

A ugust 1950, the West Indies Test at The Oval. I had only seen the famous ground from the outside during a brief Army leave in London in 1945, but my great love of cricket ensured that I knew about feats performed there by my heroes of the 1930s, and had listened on a crackling old wireless to the record-breaking innings by Len Hutton against Australia in 1938.

I applied for tickets back in May and was delighted to get seats for each day except the opening Saturday. I travelled south on the overnight train from Inverness and arrived at Euston early in the morning. I made for the ground where, at about 8 a.m., I joined other hopefuls, some of whom had queued all night and were now enjoying bacon rolls in glorious sunshine. Shortly before 11.30 a.m. we were admitted and allowed to sit on the grass between the boundary boards and the seats immediately below the gas holders.

England worked all morning for only one wicket, Bailey having Stollmeyer LBW on the stroke of lunch. One could only stand up when a wicket fell, so lunch was welcome if only to stretch one's legs. Later Rae, Worrell, Weekes and Gomez hammered the England attack to the tune of five hundred runs, but by then it was Monday and I had a more comfortable seat. Despite a wonderful 202 not out by Hutton, England lost by an innings but my summer had been made.

Since then I have watched Test cricket on all the home grounds and have been lucky enough to visit Australia and South Africa for Tests, but my first visit to The Oval still lingers among my happiest memories. Today The Oval is a magnificent all-seater stadium, but the demands of health and safety legislation dictate that fewer people can be accommodated. I sometimes wonder if those who now fill the stands, with their massive picnic hampers and drinks by the bucketful, get as much pleasure as the enthusiasts of more than forty years ago, crouching below the gasometers, munching an old fashioned sandwich and sipping a pint of bitter.

The Rt Hon the Lord Gray of Contin

The Lord Gray of Contin was MP for Ross and Cromarty between 1970 and 1983. He is a long-time supporter of Surrey CCC and a member of the All Parliamentary Cricket Group.

'BACK TO WHERE IT ALL BEGAN'

On 19 August 1953 I spent my thirteenth birthday watching England regain the Ashes. This victory was especially sweet as the winning runs were scored by my boyhood hero Denis Compton. I also remember we had to queue for hours and my father bought one of the old 'workmen's tickets' on London Underground.

Years later in December 1994, I was able to take Denis Compton back to his old school, Bell Lane School, in my constituency. When we arrived he said: 'I used to practice in front of some stumps chalked against the wall.' The stumps were still there, chalk had given way to a more permanent paint. The Head had searched the school rolls and there were the records of the young Compton playing at Lords, always accompanied by a fortunate games master! Denis explained that when he was about to leave school, Sir Pelham Warner asked his mother if he could join Middlesex; he also had the offer of a job with the local council. His mother said 'No' to Sir Pelham as she wanted him to have full-time work. Then Percy Chapman (whose daughter was to be one of his early girlfriends) asked if he could join Arsenal. Mrs Compton said: 'Four [months] plus eight equals twelve. Yes.' Thus it was Arsenal who gave us the most exciting post-war batsman.

Denis clearly enjoyed his visit to 'his roots'. He autographed his biography with the words: 'Thank you for taking me back to where it all began.' We had done so literally – as we had also seen the house where he was born and brought up!

John Marshall MP

John Marshall is MP for Hendon South.

'The Physio'

'Playing Truant'

As my father, W.H. Gunnell, was the Sports Editor of the *Birmingham Post* and my mother was a very active supporter of the local Baptist church, I was expected to combine an enthusiastic interest in sport with exemplary behaviour. My father did not believe professional detachment to be part of his duties, and as soon as sport returned after the war I was encouraged to be a fervent supporter of West Bromwich Albion FC and Warwickshire CCC. I enjoyed press access to the Hawthorns and the members' enclosure at Edgbaston. Through the double good fortune of living near the ground and my father's pass, I could easily go to the cricket when school was over.

As Warwickshire had begun the season with two away wins I was very anxious to see their first home match of 1947 against Middlesex. On Saturday 17 May, I saw my heroes dismissed by the guile of J.A. Young for only 200 but Middlesex began to lose wickets before the close of play. Desperate to see Eric Hollies crush the enemy on the following Monday, I played truant from school, keeping a low profile at the ground. Through this audacious breaking of the rules, I saw Bill Edrich score 225 in five hours fifty minutes. He drove and hooked with tremendous power and for the first time I admired the skill of an opponent. His success did not end with his innings as he opened the bowling with great energy and soon took a wicket. I was at school the next day when Warwickshire lost by an innings.

That Monday was one of the highlights of my early life. Having played truant, however, the punishment for my misdeeds was to sit in silence while my father exclaimed about the day's events, unable to boast that I had seen it all!

Footnote: *When I asked the Editor if he would like this story, he told me that he was there too, quite legitimately, in a party from Warwick School!*

John Gunnell MP

John Gunnell is MP for Morley and Leeds South and was elected in 1992. He is a keen follower of cricket and is a member of both Warwickshire CCC and Yorkshire CCC.

'DREAMS COME TRUE'

After about a twenty-year gap, I returned to playing cricket for the long-standing Lords and Commons side. In the few years I have been in Parliament, membership of the club has given me a couple of the most memorable days of my life.

Firstly, it must be every schoolboy's dream to walk out to the centre of one of our greatest cricketing arenas. My turn came in a match against the South African Ambassador's XI, the day his country re-joined the Commonwealth. The place was The Oval. A longish innings and a large bruise on my hand was all I apparently had to show for it, but it was a memory.

That memory is only matched by a game the following year, 1995, when we played the so-called Old West Indies XI. Their average age was substantially below that of the Parliamentary side. I may not have scored highly, but the entry in the scorebook: 'c. Murray b. Richards', suits me fine.

Andrew Miller MP

Andrew Miller is MP for Ellesmere Port and Neston and is an avid follower of Lancashire CCC.

'Twelfth Man'

'THE CIVIL SERVICE STRIKES BACK'

I have been bowling nondescript off-breaks for about fifty years; in fact, thinking about it, I must have achieved my 1,000 runs and 100 wickets by now! I have also been captaining the Lords and Commons team against the Mandarins (Civil Servants) for over twenty years.

For years Sir Robin Butler (the Head of the Civil Service) was their captain, although I now see he is elevated to President. Initially we used to lose badly so I soon suggested we play limited overs – thirty per side. This markedly improved our chances as their two fast bowlers could only bowl six overs each. However, we still faced a problem as we didn't have any fast bowlers of our own – to be truthful we didn't even have anyone to catch the ball reliably off the slow bowling of Robert Atkins and myself.

Fortunately, politicians initiative came to the rescue when I was asked to be Governor of my old school Bedford. I asked the master in charge of cricket if I could borrow two boys; a fast bowler and an all rounder. So for the last few years we have had what have become know as 'Morris's ringers', with the result that we usually win.

However, they are wily chaps these Mandarins, and now, at their request, the match has been put back a week. I was happy to agree, but should have thought more carefully. I spoke to the master of cricket, who said: 'Sorry, no ringers. You've moved your fixture and it clashes with exams.' So we are on our own again. We'll see – maybe we can devise some variation in the field placing that will enhance our chances!

The Rt Hon Michael Morris MP

Michael Morris, Chairman of Ways and Means and Deputy Speaker, is MP for Northampton South. He is a member of the MCC and Northamptonshire CCC. He has been a playing member of the Lords and Commons XI for over twenty years as an off-break bowler.

'Caught Behind'

'The Vicar's Tale'

Our village cricket ground happens to be church property. For this reason it is diplomatic to include the Vicar in the village XI. Unfortunately, he's a notoriously bad cricketer, though as keen as mustard. We can, of course, drop him for away matches, but we can only play home fixtures if we include him in the team. He normally bats No.11 and, when fielding, we place him wherever the ball is least likely to go.

During a recent needle match, he was fielding at long-on when the batsman, who had never been known as a big hitter, took an almighty swipe at the ball, sending it straight over the bowler's head towards the vicar. As it came towards him, straight out of the sun, everyone held their breath. Amazingly, he caught it! He was delighted. He threw the ball in the air, he threw himself on the ground, he threw his cap in the air. He applauded himself and it wasn't until nearly a minute had passed that he heard a thundering noise and saw the wicket-keeper running towards him, shouting at the top of his voice: 'Throw it in you fool, it was a no ball and they've already run eight.'

There must be a moral here for the Vicar's next sermon, but so far, I have failed to identify it.

Michael Colvin MP

Michael Colvin was elected as MP for Bristol North West in 1979. Following boundary changes he moved to Hampshire and has been MP for Romsey and Waterside since 1983. On the cricket field, he was an opening bowler for the Second Upper Club – otherwise known as Strawberry Mess – at Eton, and is a non-playing member of the Eton Ramblers.

'Crowd Control'

'GOLDEN SUMMER OF '69'

The year of 1969 saw the investiture of the Prince of Wales in Caernafon and it was the year too when Glamorgan won the County Championship.

That season there was nothing more thrilling for me than to see an innings from Majid, the twenty-two-year-old Pakistan Test player. He had been brought to Glamorgan by Wilf Wooller who was at Cambridge with his Test-player father Jahangir Khan.

Majid's batting style had rare grace and quality with the skill of an artiste. He seemed to electrify the proceedings with his free-flowing dominance at the crease.

Overall, though, it was a supreme team performance. The county had been superbly led by Tony Lewis and he had been backed up by the likes of the tireless Don Shepherd. One streak of good fortune related to the weather – they only had to play three matches in the rain-soaked month of May.

It was the second time in their history that Glamorgan had won the County Championship and they beat Worcester in fine style on 5 September at Cardiff. At the closing stages the crowd gathered round the pavillion and the rendering of *Mae Hen Wlad Fy Nhadau* was a fitting climax to a memorable occasion. They bowled their overs faster and scored their runs quicker than all the other sides of the Championship.

What a season!

Roy Hughes DL, MP

Roy Hughes has been a Member of Parliament since 1966 representing Newport until 1983, and Newport East from 1983 to the present day. He is Vice President of Glamorgan CCC and a former member of Pontllanfraith Cricket Club in Gwent.

'DEAR DIARY'

Cricket is simply the best game ever invented. I can think of no greater pleasure than spending a summer's day on a green field somewhere in the English countryside, although age and *avoirdupois* have now taken their toll. Instead I now watch avidly and thoroughly enjoy introducing the game to people from overseas. They simply cannot understand how, after five days of close fought combat, no result can be celebrated!

As far as my own memories are concerned, I was never good enough to have a string of anecdotes. I only once took more than five wickets in an innings (nine on that occasion) and only once broke fifty (both in the same game!). I once came second in the school batting competition, with an average for the season of forty-four runs, but they had to change the rules the next year since, as a bowler and batting regularly at ten or eleven, my highest score for the season was eight and I won the cricket bag prize merely because I was only out once, in sixteen innings!

My favourite entry in the cricket diary, however, was when I played in the Lords and Commons team against celebrities in a charity game run by Norman Tebbit at Lambeth Palace. Nick Scott was our captain and the opposing side contained many cricket notables from the past (and a few others). After a spirited and, as usual, short innings, I was caught on the boundary by one of the great fast bowlers of all time. The entry in my diary reads: Hanley J.J c. John Snow b. <u>Mrs Runcie</u> 16.

The Rt Hon Jeremy Hanley MP

Jeremy Hanley is MP for Richmond and Barnes. He is a member of The Lord's Taverners and describes himself as 'an opening bowler and closing batsman'.

'ALL TO AID THE THOUGHT-PROCESS'

The day after I became Minister of Public Building and Works in 1962 I went to Lord's. In between watching the cricket, which was not memorable, I pondered upon what fresh powers and responsibilities might be given to this newly named Department. Next day I drew up a list which I sent to the Prime Minister, Harold Macmillan. The Secretary to the Cabinet, Sir Norman Brook (later Lord Normanbrook) was not impressed, and it would have been duly filed away if he had not soon afterwards fallen ill. In consequence, with the help of the PM's Principal Private Secretary, Timothy Bligh (later Sir Timothy), Mr Macmillan was persuaded to use his control of the machinery of Government to take the action I wanted. Thereafter my Permanent Secretary, Sir Edward Muir, one of whose ancestors had been a pirate off the Florida Keys, entered into the Whitehall war with sundry Departments who wished to import a degree of flexibility into the guidelines. He particularly relished fierce encounters with his opposite number in the Ministry of Housing and Local Government, the formidable Dame Evelyn Sharp (later Baroness Sharp). Thus it is that any PM who spends his time watching cricket has my support – football is different, being much too frenetic and accordingly less beneficial to thought-processes.

The Rt Hon the Lord Rippon of Hexham QC

The Lord Rippon of Hexham is a member of the MCC, Surrey CCC and Somerset CCC. He has played for Somerset Stragglers, Oxford University Authentics and Hampton Wick Royal CC.

'The Loud Appeal'

'POOR SHOT SELECTION'

About forty years ago, those in the office in which I worked decided to challenge employees of another firm to a cricket match. After a great deal of difficulty, eleven people were found who were willing to participate in this event, though the cricketing credentials of at least half of our team were of a doubtful nature. One of our number in the latter category had very considerable footballing and heading skills with a tennis ball. Indeed, there was nothing that he could not do with a small ball. The other members of the team felt reassured that, because of his mastery with a tennis ball, he would prove equally skilful with a cricket ball. On the appointed day, we assembled on a village cricket pitch although, from the clothes which both teams were wearing, it was not immediately obvious that we were intending to play cricket. In due course, the game started. The team for which I was playing lost the toss and the other side decided to bat. The first three balls were very wide, but the fourth ball, purely by luck, was within the batsman's reach. He hit it very hard in the direction of our wizard with the tennis ball who saw it coming, forgot which game he was playing, and rose like a dove to head it away, meeting it beautifully with the centre of his forehead. That was the end of the game.

Sir David Knox MP

Sir David Knox is MP for Staffordshire Moorlands.

'WAITING FOR POM-POM'

There used to be times when Oxford and Cambridge Universities were able to take on county sides without fear or shame. The early 1950s were such a period. Nevertheless, although the matches were first-class, and no county side liked losing to a University, in my experience they were generally played in a friendly enough spirit – Yorkshire and the Australians being the exceptions. One such game started on 27 May 1953: Oxford University versus Middlesex at The Parks. Apart from home-grown talent, Oxford had quite a sprinkling of Rhodes Scholars, one of them being J.P. Fellow-Smith, for some reason universally known as 'Pom-Pom'. Middlesex won the toss, batted first and made 248. When our turn came, we were 91 for 3 (one of the three being myself) before Colin Cowdrey and Alan Dowding dug in for what looked to be a solid partnership. They took us to about 180 for 3 when Pom-Pom, who was next in, decided inexplicably to have a shower. Of course, no sooner was he in the shower than a wicket fell.

Law 17 says quite clearly that umpires shall allow not more than two minutes for each fresh batsman to come in. The 'note' on the Law explains that it 'is the essential duty of the captains to ensure that the in-going batsman passes the out-going before the latter leaves the field of play'. In Pom-Pom's case this was, of course, impossible. We were still feverishly putting on his pads in the pavillion when John Warr, the Middlesex captain, decided to lead his team off the field. Pom-Pom finally emerged from the pavillion in a determined manner – only to find the field empty.

It was, of course, a joke; and the umpires (Dennis Hendren and Harry Baldwin) exercised their discretion in deciding that the batting side was not guilty of 'refusing to continue play'. On all occasions thereafter, however, when Pom-Pom went to have a shower, the shout went up two or three minutes later: 'You're in, Pom-Pom!'

Lord Williams of Elvel CBE

ELECTING TO BAT

'RETIRED HURT'

The last cricket game that I played in was in an Oxfordshire village, where I appeared for the Department of Employment against the Industrial Correspondents of the press. Therefore, in my last innings in cricket I found myself walking out to partner Sir Norman Fowler, who was already at the crease. To my amazement I hit the first ball square to leg and, in reckless excitement, I decided to go for a quick single. My lack of fitness caught me out and I collapsed half way down the wicket with a torn calf muscle – my days of jumping off like a hare were over. A sympathetic fielder enabled me to crawl to the far crease before I was helped, in agony, to the boundary.

The pain and indignity of retiring hurt was made worse as I discovered that I had been pursued by the umpire. He was anxious to point out to the scorer, my wife Gillian, that the run I had achieved was a leg bye. He therefore added insult to injury by making my innings 'retired hurt 0', rather than 'retired hurt 1'! I have never disagreed with an umpire's decision more profusely and I have never felt less able to argue with it!

Needless to say, no cricket team has ever invited me to turn out for them since!

The Rt Hon Kenneth Clarke QC, MP

Kenneth Clarke, Chancellor of the Exchequer, is MP for Rushcliffe.

'The Senior Pro'

'Time, Gentleman!'

In the days when few players in the North Lancashire and District League had cars, visiting teams to Broughton-in-Furness had an arrangement whereby as soon as the church clock struck seven the match ended, so that they could catch the last train (matches at nearby Kirkby, whose pitch was on the estuary mosses, had to be timed to fit in with the high tides).

Dalton were at Broughton, and were plundered for a large total. They began their innings at 5.00 p.m. and by 6.15 p.m. were nine wickets down and over a hundred runs in deficit.

Broughton's opening bowler, a furious ginger-haired sheep farmer, had struck seven times and the sight of Dalton's last man brought him extreme pleasure. A tall, stiff, spin-bowler, the No.11 was probably the worst batsman in the league – he had never been known to score a run and had seldom made contact with the ball.

He began with a slow stroll to the wicket, took a long time digging a guard that would not have been out of place at the Somme, then asked for the sight-screen to be moved. After some minutes the bowler eagerly ran in – only to be stopped by the tail-ender who needed to clean his spectacles – and then to re-fasten his pads (which, of course, were on the wrong legs). A second run in was halted as the batsman needed the sight-screen re-adjusted and a third attempt was also halted as some fielders had apparently moved position.

By now the bowler was beside himself with fury, but the batsman had run out of excuses. In Ginger charged, and as he released the ball the church clock struck. The batsman, with the ball half way towards him, tucked the bat under his arm and strode off to the pavillion. His wickets were shattered, but the match was a draw.

Relationships between the two sides were never the same again, but the No.11 remained a popular hero in Dalton where he would often tell the story of the heroic rearguard action that saved the day for his team.

Colin Pickthall MP

Colin Pickthall is MP for West Lancashire and was elected in 1992. He was a founder member of Dalton-in-Furness CC; a founder member of Aughton CC in Lancashire and has been a member of Lancashire CCC for many years. He describes himself as a 'slow batsman and an even slower bowler', who played for Edge Hill College Staff XI for twenty-two years.

'A Question of Priority'

I remember playing for the Lords and Commons XI against the MCC at Hurlingham in the early 1970s. Lords and Commons had bowled the MCC out relatively cheaply and we were poised for victory.

As I came off the field (not out) at teatime, I was handed a message by one of the staff at Hurlingham asking that I telephone Robert Carr – the then Leader of the House, and at that time, to whom I was PPS – urgently. Ringing Robert, he told me of Reggie Maulding's resignation over the Poulson affair and added that in addition to his role as Leader of the House he had been appointed Home Secretary. He was anxious to have an immediate meeting to discuss the way in which his dual responsibilities should be handled.

I explained that Lords and Commons had an excellent chance of beating the MCC and that I was not out at the crease. He interrupted the conversation to say: 'For heaven's sake, Nick, get your priorities right. Beat the MCC and then get back here as soon as possible.' Returning to the wicket after tea, I flung my bat, notched up 93 not out, and we beat them for the first time, I believe, since the war. Robert certainly had his priorities right!

The Rt Hon Sir Nicholas Scott KBE, MP

Sir Nicholas Scott is MP for Chelsea. He is a member of the MCC, Middlesex CCC, Free Foresters, the XL Club and Leprechauns (in Ireland), and has been a playing member of the Lords and Commons Cricket Club for thirty years.

'A Defensive Prod'

'SAVING FACE'

My cricketing days are now long gone. As the pressure on my diary has increased I have found that a game of tennis is both quicker to arrange and more conveniently fitted in around the endless meetings, briefings and visits that are an inevitable part of working in politics. However, it is not without regret that I no longer have the opportunity to play cricket.

At one early stage in my cricketing career I was developing a deadly form of spin, delivered at a slow to medium pace. It worked wonders, but only lasted for a couple of games before the trick left me and I returned to unspectacular normality.

Unfortunately, my most memorable cricketing experience is not a splendid century, a devastating spell of bowling or a spectacular catch. It involves a game I played in when I was thirteen years old. I was fielding at mid-off on this occasion. For those who take no interest in cricket one of their main criticisms is that it lacks the fast-moving nature of football or rugby. I always enjoyed the games I played in, but on this particular afternoon I had been guilty of daydreaming. This is the biggest sin of the fielder. You may go hours without actually touching the ball; and then, all of a sudden, it is hurtling towards you like a cannon ball and you are faced with two choices: get out of the way, which results in complete humiliation and severely jeopardizes your place in the team; or stand your ground, take the catch and be the hero.

I chose the second option, but failed to take the catch. A missed catch is almost as humiliating as not trying at all. There is one way to avoid this, however, although it is very unpleasant. Your team mates will not be quite so hard on you for failing to hold on to a catch if the ball finds its way onto your face; and that is exactly what happened to me. The pain was great, followed by a prolonged numbness. Now I think about it, maybe not having the time isn't the real reason I gave up cricket after all.

The Rt Hon Tony Blair MP

Tony Blair, Leader of the Opposition, has been MP for Sedgefield since 1983.

'SHEER GENIUS'

I once played for the President of Cross Arrows XI against the President of MCC XI on the nursery ground at Lord's at a time when the West Indians were our visiting side that summer.

Garfield Sobers was playing on the same side as myself and during the course of the match he was handed a message saying that he would have to stand in that evening for Frank Worrell who was unwell and unable to fulfil a speaking engagement. As a result, he would have to quit the field at teatime.

At the time, he was bowling his left-arm spinners and it was the last over before tea. I was fielding at mid-off, Eric Bedser was batting at the other end. As Sobers walked back he said to me: 'This is the last ball I am going to bowl. Keep your eye on the top of the off-stump.' He loped in, bowled from the back of his hand, Bedser played forward and the off bail was removed with precision. I realised at that moment that I was in the presence of sheer cricketing genius.

The Rt Hon Sir Nicholas Scott KBE, MP

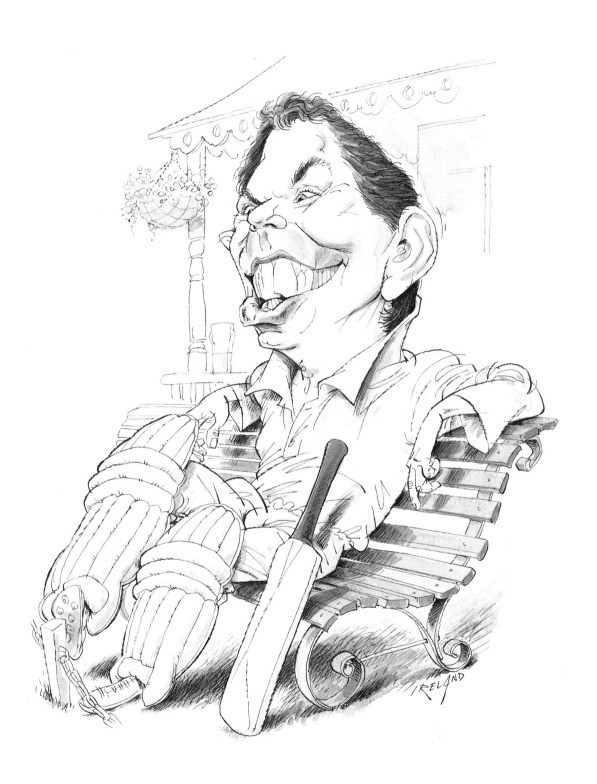

'Waiting to Bat'

'TEACHING THE BOYS A LESSON'

I decided to qualify for membership of the MCC as a playing member. This meant that I had to play ten qualifying matches. Naturally, the quality of the opposition was all-important, and for that reason, I elected to play against the Lords and Commons as being one of the MCC's easier opponents. I mean no reflection on the Lords and Commons bowling, but I do recollect that Lt. Colonel Walter Bromley-Davenport opened the bowling with his left-arm slows.

However, the next match did not go so well. MCC were playing a well-known public school. Before the game began, our captain gave us a pep talk in the pavillion: 'The boys,' he said, 'have come here to see an exhibition of batting. I don't want any messing about. I want two hundred on the board by lunch time.'

Our opening pair did rather well, and we were forty for no wicket after forty-five minutes or so. However, the opening batsman was clean bowled and so, alas, was No.3. I was batting No.4, and by the time I got to the wicket the boys were naturally crowding round the bat. I never saw the ball which took my off stump, and the bowler had achieved his hat trick.

In walked our captain. By this time, the boys were getting very excited indeed, and virtually every one of them crowded round the bat. The Colonel took guard and looked around him. 'This won't do,' he said to the umpire. 'The boys are in danger of serious injury because I hit the ball hard. I insist that they all go back ten paces.' The umpire passed the information on to the captain and, out of deference to the Colonel's seniority, the boys withdrew a few paces. In came the fast bowler, and over went the Colonel's middle stump. The opening bowler had achieved four wickets in succession, all of them clean bowled.

The Colonel was fully justified. We had indeed given an exhibition to the boys, but not quite of the kind which the Colonel had intended.

The Rt Hon Sir Peter Hordern DL, MP

Sir Peter Hordern is MP for Horsham.

'PLAYING IN DISGUISE'

One of the traditions of the Department of Employment was to organise a cricket match against the members of the industrial press who were not normally attached to the lobby. It was felt that all of us, including myself as a then Minister, should play. However, it was very many years since I had worn cricket gear and I thought I might have trouble finding some. I hit on the idea of ringing up my old friend Reg Simpson, the Nottinghamshire player, and asking him if I could borrow his kit which I thought would fit me. Indeed it did.

Having collected it from Trent Bridge, I drove to the cricket ground where the match was to be played. I donned the gear and strolled happily out to the field wearing my Nottinghamshire and England colours! It was wonderful to see the faces of the opposing team who, I am happy to say, we defeated by a very great number of runs. I scored seventeen and Jim Prior and his son scored more than fifty each.

It was a great day and I shall never forget the look on the faces of the industrial correspondents thinking they had an England player to deal with.

Sir Jim Lester MP

Sir Jim Lester has been MP for Broxtowe since 1974. He played for Car Colston CC in East Bridgford, Nottingham between 1954 and 1960 and is now Vice President of the club.

'Outside Catering'

'CAUGHT IN THE ACT'

The late Mike Noble and I told a little white lie to our then Chief Whip, Michael Cox. We both said that we had important and urgent engagements in our constituencies and would the Chief Whip allow us to be paired for the day.

The Chief Whip readily agreed to pair the two of us and both Mike and I hot-footed it up the M6 to Old Trafford to watch the game between Lancashire and Gloucester in the quarter-final of the Gillette Cup.

Mike and I were guests of the County Committee and we were sitting on the balcony watching the match when Zaheer Abbas took the Lancashire bowling apart. He hit one glorious stroke through the covers, but unfortunately for him little Johnnie Abrahams was standing there and took a superb catch. Abbas tucked his bat under his arm and disconsolately walked off the ground and up the pavillion steps. As he did so the BBC television camera tracked him and then pointed their lenses directly at the County Committee balcony where Mike Noble and I were quaffing lager. Unbeknown to us, the Chief Whip, a Gloucester man, was in his office watching the game and to his absolute astonishment saw that two of his Members of Parliament had told him a little white lie and were in fact at the cricket match and not in their constituencies on important business. Needless to say when we returned to the House of Commons our Chief Whip's remarks to us both would not be permitted to be printed in this fine book!

Roger Stott CBE, MP

Roger Stott is MP for Wigan. He is a member of Lancashire CCC, the Treasurer of the Lords and Commons Cricket Club and a member of the All Parliamentary Cricket Group.

'A First At Harrow'

I was the first woman to play cricket for the Lords and Commons cricket team at Harrow. At the dinner after the match, the captain of Harrow did not want to overtly draw attention to this breakthrough for the 'female sex' so he said: 'Welcome to Mrs Gillan, the first person to walk out to play cricket on this pitch... wearing a set of pearls.' I looked down and sure enough, there they were!

Cheryl Gillan MP

Cheryl Gillan is MP for Chesham and Amersham.

'The Tea Ladies'

'TOTAL COMMITMENT'

When captaining the Lords and Commons team against the Conservative Agents at Hurlingham, I was able, as a newly-appointed Minister at the Department of Industry, to call on two officials and the driver of my ministerial car. The value of these three mercenaries was evident at various stages of the match. Mike Tomlins, brother of the Middlesex and Gloucestershire cricketer, struck a quick and impressive thirty-three. The office driver, Gordon Phelps, conceded only eighteen runs from eight overs and, all the while, there was an unusual sharpness in Lords and Commons fielding inspired by the athletic and agile Roger Maynard (who regularly kept wicket for the Civil Service side).

There was, however, one moment when the mercenaries' contribution proved almost counter-productive and I was reminded of the hazards of occasional captaincy. Towards the end of the Agents' innings, one of their tail-enders hit the ball hard and high towards the long-off boundary. Guarding this position in front of the main body of spectators stood the ample frame of the Hon. Peter Brooke – at that time a member of the Government Whip's Office. An enthusiastic village cricketer who would later endear himself to his colleagues by appearing for publicity photographs as Chairman of the Conservative Party in Lords and Commons' cricket attire. He showed, as ever, a total commitment in keeping his eye on the ball. Unfortunately, I was also watching the ball and failed to notice the government driver making enormous speed round the boundary from long-on with his eye, too, firmly fixed on the ball. In the ensuing collision, government driver and Privy Councillor fell to the ground in thudding unison. To his undying credit, however, Peter Brooke held on to the ball and completed the catch before retiring with, happily, only minor concussion.

Sir Michael Marshall DL, MP

Sir Michael Marshall is MP for Arundel.

'A Score of Trucks'

Long ago, when I was a lad and the earth was young, I quite fancied myself as a cricketer – not quite Len Hutton standard, mind you, but getting there. Anyway, one fine day I was batting during a knockout charity competition at the local colliery in Featherstone. No batsman in the competition was to allowed to make more than twenty runs, but this became increasingly irrelevant to me as, after connecting with the first two or three balls, I was struggling. Plainly the Len Hutton touch was lacking.

I slogged on and I was heartened by the odd contact between bat and ball. I began to feel something of a hero, triumphing over cruel adversity, and I kept looking to the scoreboard for the record of my achievement. It was a traditional board with placards placed by hand and, as ever, it was in the charge of Mr Isaiah Wall, a notable Featherstone character, a man of great personal charm but scatter brains.

Putting it mildly, I was dismayed to see that Isaiah seemed unconcious of my endeavours. There was no sign of any increase in my score, meagre though it was. This began to niggle. I was out there, giving my all, but as far as Isaiah was concerned it wasn't happening. In fact, he seemed to be paying a good deal more attention to the long, heavily-laden coal trains running along the line that bordered the ground, which was the property of the colliery.

After a while I couldn't stand it any more. I had to know. 'How many?' I bellowed, in the tones of a man not to be denied, pointing at the scoreboard. 'Nineteen and a guard's van!' was the sturdy reply. Isaiah had been counting the railway trucks, not the runs! Talk about labouring in vain.

To this day that question – and that answer – still lingers in my mind. I am sure of one thing though. There were more trucks than runs!

Sir Geoffrey Lofthouse MP

Sir Geoffrey Lofthouse is MP for Pontefract and Castleford.

Electing to Bat

'One Man and His Dog'

'A Case Of Déjà-vu'

Some time in the mid-1970s a fixture was arranged between the Old Birkonian Cricket Club and the staff of King George V, Southport. This much under-publicised fixture was due to take place on a Sunday. The date was 11 June which happens to be my birthday.

We set off from Birkenhead with eleven men and an umpire, but in the intervening thirty miles we lost two people who had apparently stopped for refreshment. Accordingly at the appointed time of about 2.30 p.m. (in fact nearer 3.15 p.m.) we started with ten men. As it was my birthday I was allowed to open the innings, although my normal position would have been No.10. Not surprisingly I was bowled off-stump first ball by a long hop. This did not upset me as it was very much par for the course.

We lost wickets rapidly and at about 4.30 p.m. we were nine wickets down. In view of the importance of the date the opposing captain allowed me to have another bat. I am sure you can anticipate what happened next! I was bowled first ball, off-stump, from a long hop.

I have never submitted this to the *Guinness Book of Records*, but I think I should. There can be no more incompetent batsman.

Barry Porter MP

Barry Porter is MP for Wirral South.

'All Out!'

'THE HAND OF NELSON'

A li Bacher, captain of the all-white South African cricket tour to Britain in 1970, had every reason to see me as an enemy. For I had led the anti-apartheid campaign which had forced the tour's cancellation, ending his international career and plunging his country into more than two decades of sporting isolation.

But with the generosity of Nelson Mandela's new South Africa, he invited me to Lord's in 1994 as a guest of the Springboks for their first match in England in thirty years. I was delighted to accept – and must confess to having failed Norman Tebbit's 'cricket test' by being equally delighted at the thrilling South African victory.

In turn, I invited Ali Bacher to my constituency in July 1995 for the first ever tour by the Soweto Cricket Club. One of their matches was in the Neath Valley against Ynysygerwn.

Soweto were captained by Khaya Majola who, in his prime, would have made the South African side had he not been black. The presence of Tom Cartwright added to the sense of history coming full circle. Now the Wales Youth coach, Tom had been replaced by Basil d'Oliveira in 1968 for the England visit which, as a consequence, the South African government stopped.

Soweto and Ynysygerwn shared 444 hard-fought runs and a marvellous match was drawn on the last ball. 'There I was wondering who I wanted to win, when Nelson Mandela swooped in and made it a draw,' was my quip at the emotional post-match presentations. It had indeed seemed like divine intervention.

Peter Hain MP

Peter Hain, a left-handed batsman and leg-spinner, is MP for Neath. He was brought up in South Africa and was a leading anti-apartheid campaigner.

'UNWELCOME SUPPORT'

In 1994 Den Dover had several North West MPs playing for his MPs XI versus Chorley Cricket Club at Chorley.

One of our starring players was Social Security Minister Alastair Burt – Alastair was in charge of the Child Support Agency at the time. Prior to the match BBC North West turned up to do a bit of filming of the match which they included live into their news bulletin. We were all chuffed that our prowess on the cricket field was being given wider coverage.

Before the end of the match we noticed that the crowd was swelling somewhat and naturally thought that it was due to an influx of supporters turning up to enjoy our natural sporting ability, and wanting to get closer to the action. It was not long before our hopes were dashed when we discovered that these were not supporters but fathers and mothers who were upset by the CSA and had decided to lobby Alastair in person.

Alastair had every reason not to be caught out or bowled, but when he was finally dismissed he was clapped out by his fellow MPs only to be greeted by CSA cases who demanded instant attention at the side of the field.

After that time we never told the BBC when our matches were being played.

Nigel Evans MP

Nigel Evans is MP for Ribble Valley. He is a member of the All Parliamentary Cricket Group, but admits to only playing once a year for Den Dover's XI against Chorley Cricket Club. Last year's appearance resulted in an innings of four – a vast improvement he says on the previous year's performance when 'I was clean bowled for a duck by a twelve-year-old'.

'UNFORGIVABLE ERROR'

In my early teens I used to go to the nets at our Wath-upon-Dearne Athletic Ground. Boys were coached by two elderly miners who had been local stars for many years. There were tennis courts of a kind behind the scoreboard but no one played. Cricket was the game and Yorkshire commanded great allegiance.

At last I was picked to play for Wath in the South Yorkshire League. Off we went to play Hoyland St. Peters. They bowled ferociously and our wickets fell rapidly. I survived numerous close calls. At the end I was twelve not out – our top scorer. Hoyland beat us but not by very many runs.

The *South Yorkshire Times*, our local weekly, used to report all the South Yorkshire League matches in full. I took an enormous interest in the local press the following Friday. When the paper arrived I turned immediately to the cricket results expecting to read that I had been Wath's top scorer. Instead I read that my friend, T. Heany, was reported to have scored my runs. I rejoiced for him. However, I do not think any subsequent newspaper inaccuracy, distortion or omission has given me cause for equal disappointment.

Still, whilst I recall the error I can remember that I was once top scorer for our local side whilst I was still quite young.

Peter Hardy MP

Peter Hardy is MP for Wentworth.

'In the Slips'

'GETTING YOUR OWN BACK'

It is a tribute to how quickly and peacefully events have developed in South Africa that only a few years ago it would have been impossible to imagine an official England cricket tour of that country.

We should not overlook the role that anti-apartheid activists played since the 1960s in campaigning against sporting involvement with the old régime. It all started on 26 June 1965 when I led the first demonstration in Britain against a touring South Africa side. The venue was Queen's Ground in Chesterfield where a number of us, including a very young Derbyshire miner called Dennis Skinner, mounted a picket line brandishing 'Apartheid Isn't Cricket' banners.

The picket that day was a resounding success, but it caused some upset to an aspiring young sports reporter, now doyenne of all commentators, Stuart Hall. Disappointed at the lack of cricket to observe and obliged to interview the demonstrators, he decided to get his own back on the Radio Newsreel that evening.

In an attempt to downgrade the importance of the demonstration, he described me as being dressed in a sharp grey bespoke waistcoated suit with blue-buttoned collared shirt and red tie who once boxed for Oxford. He added: 'With Mr Pendry was *Z Cars* actor Stacy Davis, who had to leave at lunchtime as his Manx cat had given birth to five kittens.'

Although absolutely true he managed to reduce a successful demonstration to a nothing event on radio. Despite this Stuart has gone on to find fame and fortune in sports broadcasting. He is now one of my closest friends and is even godfather to my daughter.

Tom Pendry MP

Tom Pendry is MP for Stalybridge and Hyde.

'DUTCH COURAGE'

Watching cricket in The Parks in Oxford is a pastime that depends, more than ordinarily, on the weather. The contrast between an April day of icy winds and scudding rain, and a May day of bright sunshine and gentle breezes is especially stark. As a life-long supporter of Hampshire, who regularly play the University in the early season, I have known and loved The Parks in all weathers. Yet it is hard to beat this ground on a hot June afternoon.

In 1968, Hampshire brought Barry Richards to The Parks for the first time. As it happened, my visit coincided with a party to celebrate the end of a friend's final exams. After consuming a great deal of champagne at Keble, my friend and I 'walked' his girlfriend back to Lady Margaret Hall, where she was due to rehearse Aristophanes's *The Frogs*. Leaving her propped against a hedge for support, we made our way to the pavillion to watch Barry Richards's tutorial in the art of batsmanship.

The effect of the champagne had not worn off, and my limbs were curiously immobile. My brain, however, was still functioning in a lazy, hazy way and, in due course, I noticed that the ball had been hit hard and high, and was heading my way. My brain registered that it would land on or near me, but my limbs ignored the signals which my brain now began to send, urgently. To cut a long, slow story short, the ball landed on the bench beside me, inches away. Those nearby marvelled at my *sangfroid*, never realising that my *sang* was not so much *froid* as diluted.

Clearly a case of premature by-election fever, but it taught me not to mix cricket and champagne, at least until after the match.

Simon Coombs MP

Simon Coombs is MP for Swindon.

'Fog Stopped Play And Other Tales'

Both my grandfathers and father were keen club cricketers in their time and I seem to have played cricket avidly from the moment when I could stand upright and hold a tiny bat. As a result, so many incidents come to mind that it is difficult to choose only one or two. However, I particularly remember the amusement I got as a boy when I bowled an apple at my father, instead of the ball, in my grandmother's garden in Norfolk, and saw his surprise as the 'ball' disintegrated as he hit it; also an occasion many years later, on tour with Nondescripts CC at Happisburgh in Norfolk, when a sea fret rolled in and 'fog stopped play' was succeeded in the scorebook by 'match abandoned due to fog' (fielding in the covers I could no longer see the stumps when we came off, never mind the pavillion!).

Along with these I would place my happy years playing for Canewdon CC (once carrying my bat), Access CC in Essex, Sutton Coldfield CC and Stockton CC in Warwickshire (best bowling so far in my career, five wickets for three runs), and Romany CC in Yorkshire, when late one evening Romany won the midweek evening cup – our celebrated stonewaller hitting a six off the last ball to secure an unlikely victory.

My personal highlights so far have to be, however, playing for the Commons against the Lords at The Oval for the first time in 1993, and coming off at tea as one of the 'not out' batsman with David Faber MP (who later went on to get eighty-odd whilst I got thirty-four) to be greeted by the Prime Minister at the boundary edge, and later the same glorious summer getting fifty-four, opening the batting at a match at Abbey Village CC in Lancashire, with my two young sons operating the score box.

Nick Hawkins MP

Nick Hawkins is MP for Blackpool South.

'Retired Hurt'

'MISSED OPPORTUNITY'

I n cricket as in politics aspiration often exceeds achievement. Not having made the First XI at school I opted for the river at Cambridge and made only occasional appearances for a social cricket team known as the Pagans.

However, the opportunity to play for the Lords and Commons against Westminster School in 1988, where my son was in the First XI, was too tempting to resist.

Lords and Commons batted first and did not distinguish themselves although as a middle order batsman I made a modest contribution. After tea, the Westminster School opening pair threatened to knock off the runs needed with embarrassing ease and so, as it was rather early, some wickets were sacrificed in order to entertain players and spectators alike.

This eventually brought my occasional medium pace into action from the Vauxhall Bridge Road end. To the surprise of everyone, most of all myself, I obtained two wickets with consecutive balls dismissing Westminster School players who were presumably hoping for advancement in the Conservative Party.

I had never had a hat trick in my life and therefore with the enthusiastic support of the captain, the new batsman was crowded with fielders. Our most senior player was an elderly peer whose prowess on the field had been formidable for more than sixty years, but who was no longer an agile mover. I therefore placed him at gully, calculating that this was the least likely place for the batsman to hit the off break I planned to deliver.

Alas, the new batsman dollied up to gully the sort of catch which doting grandparents offer eighteen-month-old infants when teaching them to play with a ball. To my eternal disappointment and to the elderly peer's embarrassment the ball flew gently into his hands and thence to the ground. My one chance of a hat trick had passed for ever.

Tim Yeo MP

Tim Yeo is MP for Suffolk South.

'WAITING FOR THE CALL'

One idyllic summer's day more than thirty years ago, in that distant epoch of my life when I could occasionally score runs, I was a guest player in an Invitation XI which took on a village side in Hertfordshire.

The pitch was hard and true, the bowling mediocre and I had been in good form in recent matches. Runs were there for the asking and I was full of confidence.

I soon discovered that my opening partner, whom I had not previously met, suffered from a speech impediment. When he struck the ball between fielders his 'Yer... yer... yer' eventually clarified into 'Yes' and his 'Ner... ner... ner' became 'No' when he declined to run.

Frustrated by the number of quick singles which we were missing, I eventually decided not to wait for the final pronouncement, 'Yer... yer... yer' or 'Ner... ner... ner', was good enough for me.

Foolish me! The moment came when he struck the ball square of the wicket. 'Yer... yer... yer' he called and off I ran. Half way down the wicket, to my horror, I realised that he was still rooted to the ground. That very moment his 'Yer... yer... yer' clarified into 'Your call!'

I was run out by yards. Players, umpires spectators and scorers collapsed with laughter. Many minutes passed before normal play was resumed.

Andrew Hunter MP

Andrew Hunter is MP for Basingstoke.

'Silly Mid-off'

'NEEDS MUST'

I am not a cricketer but now that I represent a cricketing county my latent love of the game has flowered!

When I first met John Major and he realised I was the prospective parliamentary candidate for Worcester, he interrogated me fiercely about my interest in cricket. I tried to explain that having been brought up in Berkshire which was not sadly a first-class county, I was trying my best to improve my knowledge of the game.

The Prime Minister was not impressed: 'Berkshire – home of Peter May, one of the finest cricketers this country has ever produced.' He proceeded to reel off what seemed to me to be the whole of Peter May's *Wisden* entry and so my first meeting with the Prime Minister was not the unqualified success I might have hoped!

Even now my visits to New Road are not as frequent as I would like and my knowledge hasn't improved greatly. I certainly intend to avoid engaging the Prime Minister in a meaningful discussion on the subject of cricket for the sake of my future career!

Peter Luff MP

Peter Luff is MP for Worcester.

'The Spin Bowler'

'CARRY ON, CAPTAIN'

The Stanmore 3rd XI captain of fifteen to twenty years ago was well known for his eccentricity. At that time, the 3rd XI used to play on one of the pitches at Whitchurch playing fields (now a school). As there was more than one pitch, it follows that there was often more than one game going on, and on one famous occasion our hero had got through the first half of the game before he realised he was playing the wrong opposition; there was then insufficient time to restart the game against the correct opposition, and so the match continued.

On another occasion, Stanmore had been fielding for more than an hour before the opposing captain noticed that we had twelve men on the field! This was eclipsed a few weeks later when we took the field with two wicket-keepers. One of the players pointed out the error, only to be met with the rebuke: 'Be quiet, I'm the captain.' In spite of apparently doing most things wrong, from a cricketing point of view, our hero had a record as captain of Stanmore's 3rd XI which was second to none in recent times.

Hugh Dykes MP

Hugh Dykes was first elected for Harrow East in 1970. The last time he played cricket was in 1968, but he goes to Lord's three times a year and describes himself as a 'nervous' member of the Lords and Commons Cricket Club.

'The Scorer'

'A Dying Breed'

I was fortunate enough to be taken in hand by a leading player at the Grammar School I attended and was taught, at the tender age of thirteen, the skills of a leg-spinner, which came naturally to me. With a supple wrist and strong fingers it was easy for me to turn the ball by a yard from leg to off or to deceive the batsman with a googly that turned as much the other way.

I played for years in the school First XI and won the bowling prize in my final year at Manchester Grammar School. It was not unsual for me to be brought on early in an innings and then to come back to mop up the tail, recording some staggering figures. However, in the 1950s leg-spinners were fairly commonplace and certainly not a rare breed.

With one or two games for Manchester University and regular league appearances in the Liverpool Competition, I improved my batting and still kept my hand in at leg-spinning throughout the 1960s. During the 1970s I was too busy working in the construction industry and winning my way into Westminster to spend any time at all playing cricket. It was a tremendous pleasure in 1981, after a couple of years in the House, to bowl my first ball for more than a decade. The first delivery was a classic leg break which pitched on middle and leg and spun away breaking nearly a yard to the off. The regular umpire for the Lords and Commons turned to me in astonishment and said, 'Was that a leg break?' 'Yes, of course,' I said in a matter of fact way. 'That is the first one I have seen for fifteen years,' he remarked.

Since then I have been delighted to perform as often as possible for the Lords and Commons and have sometimes had to fill a gap as a stock bowler, but my personal delight is in bowling leg breaks and googlies – including the occasional top-spinner. What's more, my dream has come true in that leg-spinning is again all the rage with Shane Warne being one of the idols of present-day cricket.

I still maintain that a leg-spinner can dismiss top-order batsmen as well as run through a tail more quickly than any other type of bowler. Indeed, in the 1995 season, I had the unusual experience of dismissing two century-makers who had together knocked up over 200 for an opening partnership. I will not divulge my bowling figures for that day – for obvious reasons. It is never easy to maintain a good line and length and economical figures are difficult to achieve from what is a very precise art form!

Den Dover MP

Den Dover is MP for Chorley.

'THE NOVICE'

The MP played, on the magnificent county ground, in the captain of England's side against the Archbishop's XI. The aim was to raise thousands of pounds for charity and at stake was prestige and pride.

The Archbishop bowled in the heat of the summer day and took no wickets. Others came, and went, and the MP was padded up and in to bat. It was his first, and only, time on the hallowed square. He intended to make the most of it.

He took guard and faced the county schoolboy bowling for the Archbishop. He survived four balls, which he did not see, and edged the fifth into the waiting hands of the slips.

Back in the pavillion he turned, apologetically, to the captain:

'I've never played that badly before,' he said.

'Oh,' said the captain coldly, 'You've played before, have you.'

Roger Gale MP

Roger Gale is MP for Thanet North.

'The Umpire'

'MINOR COUNTY BLUES'

Being brought up in the War, and being a natural hooligan, gave me the excuse to pay little attention to school work – with the result that by the time I was eleven years old, I was what might be called trouble. Then, quite by chance, I found I could play football and cricket, and although I had more natural ability for football, my first love was cricket.

My cricket career went from playing for Edmonton schoolboys to Middlesex schoolboys, to the South of England schoolboys (at the age of fifteen, breaking the record at Edmonton Cricket Club, which still stands, at 193) to a professional career (albeit short-lived) at Gloucester and Warwickshire. This ran alongside a professional football career at Aston Villa.

I returned at the age of twenty-eight, out of work, to my home in London, and pursued a club career with Edmonton where I became captain. I also became captain of the Club Cricket Conference which represents 3,500 clubs in the south of England.

By the time I reached thirty I was playing my best cricket. Hertfordshire was allowed four special registrations for people who lived outside the county, and after much discussion between Middlesex and Hertfordshire County Cricket Clubs, I was one of the four chosen to play under special registration. Hertfordshire-born club players who wanted to play for the county, very much resented special registration players because they clearly took up places in the team that they might otherwise have filled.

My first major event came amidst much publicity and glory, and was against Bedfordshire. Playing for them at that time were the ex-Notts fast bowler Ian Davidson, the ex-Notts wicket-keeper Geoff Millman. The side was captained by Jack Smith who was regarded as one of the very best tacticians in the minor county game. At a west Hertfordshire cricket club where the game was being played on a bright Tuesday morning, Hertfordshire won the toss, and at 11.30, D. Evans walked out to bat with Geoff Smith, a former Essex county player. The first ball I received at twenty-nine minutes to twelve was a bouncer, which I fended off, only to be caught by the wicket-keeper. I was out for nought, second ball, caught Millman, bowled Davidson.

In the second innings the following day, I walked out to bat, and Mr Smith, well aware that this was my first match, said to me as I walked to the wicket: 'I hope you have been practising facing bouncers.' I made no comment, and the third ball in my second innings was another bouncer. The result caught Millman, bowled Davidson – a pair in my first match.

I did not play for Hertfordshire for another four years, but eventually returned, at the age of thirty-two, and played thirty matches, eventually winning a county cap when I slogged fifty in twenty minutes to get Hertfordshire into the Gillette Cup

David Evans MP

David Evans is MP for Welwyn Hatfield.

'NEVER LATE'

The Prime Minister shows a tremendous interest in sport which is very good. He loves his cricket and is a fanatic. If he were at a match where I was umpiring, he would always come to see me in the dressing room during lunch or tea, to have a few words and to see how I was. I thought it was wonderful for a Prime Minister to do that and I really appreciated it.

I had an invitation from the Prime Minister to visit him at Chequers. As many people know I am always early for appointments. When I was invited for lunch with the Queen at Buckingham Palace, I got there at 8.30 in the morning. It was the same at Chequers. I was invited for one o'clock but I arrived there at 7.30 in the morning and found myself just walking around outside the main gates, passing the time. Eventually, the police officers phoned through to say I was there and the Prime Minister said: 'Well, if it's Dickie, send him down.' So I sat with John and Norma Major for a couple of hours in the morning just talking about cricket. Then we had a magnificent buffet – it was a day I shall remember for the rest of my life.

Harold 'Dickie' Bird MBE

'CHANGING FORTUNES'

By now, I am no newcomer to the House of Commons. There is, of course, a strong passion for cricket within Parliament. This stems largely from the Prime Minister who is often seen at England matches. On his elevation to the Chancellor's office some years ago, he was introduced to the players: John Morris, formerly of England now of Durham, will no doubt boast to his team mates of meeting the future Prime Minister dressed only in his jockstrap. Occasionally Kenneth Clarke, a former Health Minister, is seen on the Committee balcony at Nottingham enjoying what seems to be a relaxing lager or two and a packet of fags.

My first appearance at the House was shortly prior to our departure to the West Indies in 1994. We were there to meet the All Parliamentary Cricket Group, and the drinks just preceded Prime Minister's questions. Mark Ramprakash was engaged in earnest conversation with an elderly, white-haired gentleman and asked him if he would be asking the Prime Minister anything that afternoon. Sadly, for Ramps, the gentleman in question was Ossie Wheatley, chairman of the TCCB cricket committee!

More recently I addressed the All Parliamentary Cricket Group, encouraged to do so by a strong Lancastrian contingent. It was shortly after the World Cup and, in jest, I likened the England team to the Conservative party: tired, low in morale, down in the opinion polls with the country crying out for change. Fortunately, I think, our fortunes are now on the up...!

Michael Atherton

ACKNOWLEDGEMENTS

Many thanks to the Prime Minister, the Leader of the Opposition and all my parliamentary colleagues who have taken time to share their cricketing memories and to Mike Atherton and Dickie Bird for their contributions. My thanks also to John Ireland for his splendid caricatures and a final special thanks to Taylor Woodrow who have helped to make this book possible.

Harry Greenway MP